WHO WOULD WIN?®

POLAR BEAR

VS.

GRIZZLY BEAR

BY
JERRY PALLOTTA

ILLUSTRATED BY
ROB BOLSTER

Scholastic Inc.

New York Toronto London Auckland
Sydney Mexico City New Delhi Hong Kong

The publisher would like to thank the following for their kind permission to use their photographs in this book:

Page 14: © John Warden / AlaskaStock.com; page 15: © Alaska Stock Images / National Geographic Stock; page 20: Courtesy of Dave Newbury, Department of Anatomy / University of Bristol; page 21: Courtesy of Cooper Landing Museum; page 22: © Miles / Corbis; page 23: © Michio Hoshino / Minden Pictures

Thank you to my research assistants, Olivia Packenham and Will Harney.
And thank you to author Shelley Gill for a zillion bear stories.

—*J.P.*

To my "Running Bear," Luke.

—*R.B.*

ISBN 978-93-5471-175-6

This reprint edition : September 2024
Printed in India

Book design by Rob Bolster

During the Arctic winter, polar bears and grizzly bears live far away from each other. But during the summer months, while looking for food, polar bears and grizzly bears sometimes end up in the same location.

What would happen if they met each other? What would happen if they had a fight? Who would win?

SCIENTIFIC NAME OF POLAR BEAR
"Ursus maritimus"

Meet the polar bear. Polar bears are considered sea mammals. They spend most of their time on the frozen sea. They prefer to live near the edge of the ice pack. They are the largest of all bears.

FUN FACT

There are no polar bears in Antarctica.

REMEMBER

Polar bears: North Pole.
Penguins: South Pole.
There are no penguins in the Arctic.

SCIENTIFIC NAME OF GRIZZLY BEAR
"Ursus arctos horribilis"

Meet the grizzly bear. Grizzly bears are mammals that live on land. You can tell grizzlies by the huge hump at their shoulders. This is a muscle they use for digging.

DID YOU KNOW?

There are no grizzly bears in the southern hemisphere.

Sorry, black bear. You are not in this book because you are not as big and ferocious as grizzlies and polar bears.

FUN FACT

While on a hunting trip, President Teddy Roosevelt refused to shoot an old bear. Newspapers teased him, and from then on cute stuffed toy bears were called "teddy bears."

FUN FACT

Male bears are called boars. Female bears are called sows.

Forget about it, giant panda. You are a plant eater and are no match for a polar bear or a grizzly.

Polar bears have snow-white fur. Their color allows them to blend in with their environment—snow, slush, and ice.

FUN FACT

Polar bears have black skin.

POLAR BEAR NAMES

Ice bear, nanook, white bear, sea bear

DID YOU KNOW?

A polar bear's white fur is actually translucent. Translucent means see-through or clear.

Grizzly bears come in four different colors: dark brown, brown, reddish brown, and blond.

FUN FACT
Grizzlies are also called *silvertips.*

These colors allow grizzlies to blend in with their environment—fallen leaves, dirt, rocks, and trees.

TEN FEET

DID YOU KNOW?

The polar bear is an apex predator. An apex predator is an animal that has no natural enemies.

INTERESTING FACT

Polar bears can stand on their hind legs.

Polar bears are the largest predatory land animals. Polar bears can grow to be ten feet tall. Here is a kindergartner next to a polar bear.

EIGHT FEET

FUN FACT

Grizzlies can also stand on their hind legs.

A grizzly bear can stand eight feet tall. They tower over you.

A polar bear paw is larger than this book.

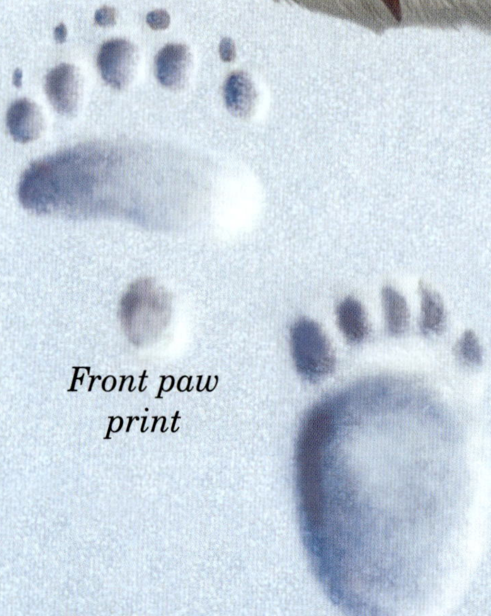

Front paw print

Back paw print

DID YOU KNOW?

A polar bear paw is slightly webbed. It is like an oar—perfect for swimming.

REMEMBER

If you ever see polar bear footprints, pay attention! Inupiak people say, "You never see the one that gets you."

This is a grizzly track. A track is a footprint. Their front claws can be four inches long.

Front paw track

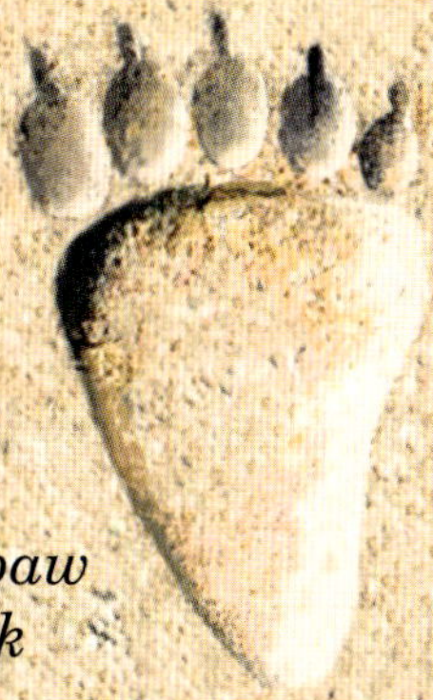

Back paw track

FUN FACT

Humans have nails on their fingers and toes. Bears have claws. Each paw has five long, sharp claws.

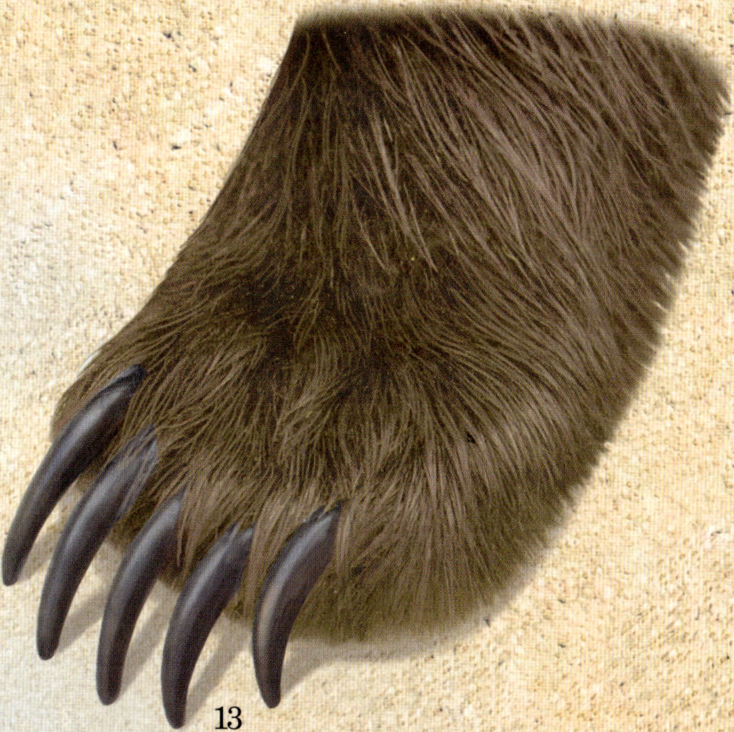

Polar bears are excellent swimmers. They can swim farther than fifty miles at one stretch.

Polar bears mostly eat meat from the ocean—walrus, seals, sea lions, and fish. Seals are their favorite food.

Fun Fact

Polar bears do the dog paddle.

Did You Know?

YIKES! A polar bear can eat a human, but it hardly ever happens. Not many people live near polar bears.

Grizzly bears are good swimmers, but they prefer standing in a river to catch fish. If a grizzly stands in the right spot, a migrating salmon might jump right into its mouth.

Interesting Fact

Grizzlies eat salmon, trout, apples, berries, honey, and anything they can get their paws on. Grizzlies have also been known to eat moose, elk, caribou, rodents, sheep, grubs, and clams.

Not a Fun Fact

Each year grizzlies eat a few people.

Open wide! Polar bears have carnivore teeth—canine teeth in front and huge molars in back.

IMPORTANT FACT

Polar bears can smell a seal through ice three feet thick.

FUN FACT

"Carnivore" means "meat eater."

Grizzly bears have teeth that are similar to a polar bear's.

Grizzlies have such a good sense of smell that they can detect a dead animal ten miles away.

A polar bear can run twenty-five miles per hour. That is faster than a human can run. Polar bears can run down some caribou!

So who would win if they had a fight? The polar bear or the grizzly bear?

Grizzly bears look slow. But don't be fooled. Grizzly bears can easily outrun a human. They are fast!

DID YOU KNOW?

A grizzly is faster on land. A polar bear is probably faster on ice.

Here is a polar bear skeleton.

GOOFY FACT
All polar bears are left-handed.

INTERESTING FACT
The sun bear from Asia grows to be only about five feet tall, the average height of a human.

Bear skeletons are somewhat similar to a human's. Four limbs, five fingers, five toes, backbone, ribs, head, neck, and hips.

Here is the complete skeleton of a grizzly bear.

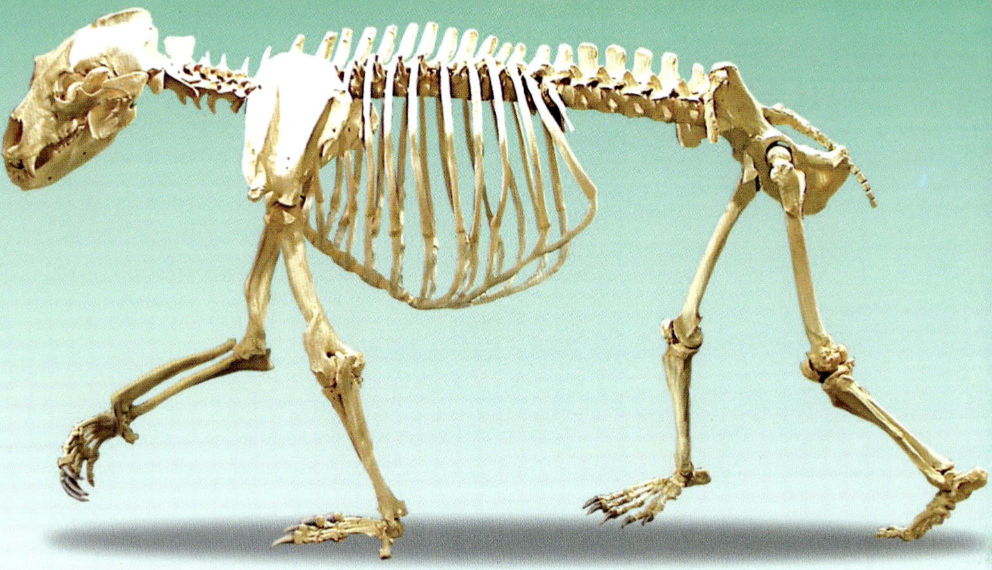

SAD FACT

The silver bear from Mexico was hunted to extinction.

INTERESTING FACT

Scientists have studied bear DNA and think that the polar bear and the grizzly bear are descended from the same animal. Both adapted to their environments. Polar bears prefer the sea. Grizzlies prefer to live on land. Only an expert osteologist, a bone scientist, can tell their bones apart.

Polar bears are solitary animals. They rarely fight each other, and mostly they stay away from each other.

Grizzly bears are also solitary animals. But groups of grizzlies sometimes fish together during a salmon migration.

Male polar bears do not hibernate. They spend all winter looking for food. They might build a snow cave to sleep away an unusually bad storm.

Female polar bears build a "maternity den," usually in the snow and ice, to spend the winter and take care of their cubs. This conserves the mom's energy.

DID YOU KNOW?

Hibernation is when an animal goes into a resting state of inactivity, with a slower heartbeat, no eating or drinking, and a lower body temperature.

Just before winter, grizzlies eat as much as they can to fatten up for a long sleep. Grizzly bears have a deep winter sleep, but it is not true hibernation. A grizzly can wake up and suddenly attack you. In the springtime, grizzlies are hungry. Watch out!

FUNNY POLAR BEAR STORIES

A US Navy nuclear sub surfaced in the Arctic ice, only to find a few polar bears snooping around.

Sometimes polar bears take naps in the funniest of positions.

A famous nature photographer waited for days to get a good picture of a polar bear. He was eating lunch in his pickup truck one day when he saw a big surprise in his rearview mirror.

FUNNY GRIZZLY BEAR STORIES

An Alaskan man came home to find a grizzly bear relaxing in his jacuzzi.

A sailor anchored in a harbor in Alaska was awakened by a noise. He found a grizzly walking around his yacht. Scared out of his wits, he pushed the grizzly off with an oar.

Using a cheeseburger, a tourist lured a grizzly bear into his car. The foolish man wanted to get a nice picture of the bear sitting with his wife. The woman screamed, and the confused bear ran away.

It is summer.

A polar bear steps off the ice onto a beach. A grizzly bear comes out of the woods.

They see each other. They can smell each other. Both bears stand to get a better look. Then it happens. The grizzly charges at the polar bear, growling and showing his teeth.

The polar bear crouches down, paws up, ready for battle. Running at full speed, the grizzly knocks over the polar bear.

The polar bear gets right up and fights back. Whap! He smacks the grizzly in the face. Ouch! They claw, scratch, and bite. It’s a nasty fight.

They wrestle, each trying to get the advantage.

Rolling around, both bears get dirty from the sand and mud.

The grizzly is relentless—it keeps on fighting!

Suddenly, the polar bear sees no point in fighting anymore. There is no reason to fight to the death. The polar bear runs away.

The grizzly wins. But now he is sore and tired. He hopes he never runs into a polar bear again. These two bears are so similar—next time the outcome could be quite different!

WHO HAS THE ADVANTAGE?

CHECKLIST

POLAR BEAR		GRIZZLY BEAR
☐	Size	☐
☐	Claws	☐
☐	Hunting Skill	☐
☐	Teeth	☐
☐	Sense of Smell	☐
☐	Speed	☐
☐	Family	☐
☐	Hibernation	☐